Ozzy – Famous rock star and pioneer of heavy metal. Doesn't he dye his hair red – despite being over 50?

Sharon – Charming and boisterous. Occasionally outrageous. Has been known to chuck ham over the neighbour's fence.

The kids – Kelly and Jack. Rich but real. They may party with celebs, but they still get spots!

Prepare to meet . . . *the Osbournes.*

Scholastic Children's Books
Commonwealth House, 1-19 New Oxford Street
London WC1A 1NU, UK
a division of Scholastic Ltd
London ~ New York ~ Toronto ~ Sydney ~ Auckland
Mexico City ~ New Delhi ~ Hong Kong

First published in paperback in the US by Scholastic Inc., 2002
First published in paperback in the UK by Scholastic Ltd, 2002

Text copyright © Scholastic Inc., 2002

ISBN 0 439 97884 X

Printed and bound in Great Britain by
Cox & Wyman Ltd, Reading, Berkshire

2 4 6 8 10 9 7 5 3 1

The publishers would like to thank the following sources for their kind
permission to reproduce the pictures in this book:

Front cover: **Top**: Robert Matheu/Retna Ltd; **Bottom left**: Scott Gries/Image Direct;
Bottom right: Scott Gries/Image Direct;
Colour insert: **Pg 1**: Everett Collection; **Pg 2**: (top) T. Smith/Camera Press;
(bottom) John Kelly/Retna Ltd; **Pg 3**: T. Tan/Shooting Star; **Pg 4**: (top) Sara De Boer/Retna
Ltd; **Pg 5**: Scott Gries/Image Direct; **Pg 6**: (top) Luis Martinez/Retna Ltd; (bottom) Barbara
Binstein/Image Direct; **Pg 7**: Tammie Arroyo/Retna Ltd;
Pg 8: Scott Gries/Image Direct

An unauthorised biography
by Kord Miller

✠ CONTENTS

✠ CHAPTER ONE
Welcome to Planet Osbourne!

The American TV Nation has a new First Family! A family whose members have captured the imaginations and tickled the funny bones of young Americans everywhere.

Dad is a rich rock star, and if he's got a concert to play, then Mum — savvy, charming and occasionally outrageous — will take care of the travel plans. The kids are real, quirky, stylish and cool teenagers who fight, laugh and love music and each other. They all have minds of their own and don't mind letting everyone know what they're thinking. They don't have to please anyone, and yet they seem to please everyone. Who doesn't envy them?

What's more, this favourite American family isn't even American – they're British! They're the Osbournes, of course, the stars of their own hilarious real-life TV series – and now they're taking the UK by storm, too!

Music lovers (and reporters) the world over agreed: Ozzy Osbourne stole the show at the monster concert in June 2002 celebrating the Queen's Golden Jubilee. When Ozzy came on stage to sing 'Paranoid', hundreds of thousands of fans watching the show live from Buckingham Palace and on giant TV screens along the Mall chanted: 'Ozzy! Ozzy!' Only Her Majesty got a bigger ovation. Other great British rock stars like Eric Clapton and Joe Cocker received only polite applause. Even the legendary Paul McCartney didn't get the crowd to shout their love for him like Ozzy did. And hundreds of millions of viewers around the world saw

Princes William and Harry clapping in time during Ozzy's performance.

Hosting the US telecast was none other than Sharon Osbourne, whose genuine awe at the event, plus her famous sense of humour and timing, received unqualified raves. 'She's a natural to host next years Oscars,' said the chief of a major TV network – not bad for Sharon's debut as a television presenter.

The Osbourne family has lived in small rural villages, where the children – that's Kelly and Jack – were sometimes taunted on the way to school about their outrageous father. They've lived in London as well, and recently they relocated to a Spanish-style mansion in Beverly Hills, Los Angeles. They are currently the most famous residents of their already famous neighbourhood and they just happen to hang out in West Hollywood, where all the action is. Bring on the Osbournes – they rule!

America's First 'Reality TV' Family

In 1972, the Loud family from Santa Barbara, California, allowed a camera crew into their home and into their lives for several months. The three hundred hours of film was shot and edited down into twelve episodes, which ran as An American Family. The prosperous and attractive Louds, with their five teenage children, became a national sensation. But TV viewers seemed divided between those who were horrified that a family would allow their private lives to be shown on television, and those who couldn't get enough. Sound familiar?

How It All Began

Last year, when MTV visited the new Osbourne family home for an episode of *Cribs*, a show that goes into the homes of rock stars, the audience response was 'incredible,' according to an MTV spokesperson. So the channel asked the Osbournes if they could focus on their everyday life for an unscripted series. Crews arrived in September 2001 and filmed a few weeks into the New Year.

Living with the cameras was an adjustment for the family. Remembering the first days, Kelly has said that she thought early on about using more 'ladylike' language, but she soon just started being herself. The cameras became a part of her life, but after a while she wished they'd just pack up and leave.

Filming the programme has been an incredible ride, involving lots of ups as well as downs. Join the ride and learn what's ahead in the TV season to come. And that's not all: you'll also discover what it *really* feels like to be part of the world's new favourite family!

Is It Really 'Reality'?

Is The Osbournes pure reality? Of course not — there are no hidden cameras in the Osbourne mansion, and not one second of tape gets shown on TV without the approval of the show's executive producer — who happens to be Sharon! No one as smart as Sharon would let anyone in her family look bad to the world. She makes sure audiences are always laughing with the four stars, and never at them.

One of Sharon's rules is, the children cannot be seen doing anything that might embarrass them — now or later! And it's not just what you don't see, because what you do see is really there very deliberately. It's supposed to make you laugh and cheer and take sides with your new friends who belong to a real/fantasy family. In short, insiders call it great television.

✠ CHAPTER TWO
Professionally Known as: Ozzy Osbourne

Ozzy Osbourne's story is larger than life. He is one of rock 'n' roll's biggest and most enduring stars. And since March 5, 2002, he's become one of TV's biggest stars, too. Entertainment columnists rank him among the world's ten most famous celebrities.

Born in 1948 in Birmingham, one of six children, John Michael Osbourne ('Ozzy' was courtesy of schoolmates) remembers a childhood when there were two bedrooms for eight people, and in his wardrobe just one pair of shoes, socks and trousers, and just one jacket.

His first ambition was to be a plumber and at fifteen he became a plumber's asssistant.

His next ambition, once he heard the Beatles, was to be one of them.

The Early Years

Unfortunately, Ozzy's salary from unclogging drainpipes didn't exactly buy the mid-sixties swinging London lifestyle of a young Paul McCartney or Mick Jagger.

So, like many a teenager before him, he decided to sing his way to the top. At school he'd performed in some classic English operettas and found he had an impressive singing voice and a gift for dramatic flair. Ozzy's next step was joining a band. Make that a lot of bands – with embarrassing names like Black Panthers, Music Machine, Approach, Rare Breed, Mythology, The Polka Tulk Blues Band and Earth.

He is best known, however, for the band he formed in the late sixties called Black Sabbath.

Named after a scary 1935 Boris Karloff movie (it was also the title of the band's first single), Black Sabbath was an instant sensation, and it was later credited with inventing heavy metal rock. With Ozzy on lead vocals (and harmonica!), Black Sabbath also included Tony Iommi on guitar, Bill Ward on drums and Geezer Butler on bass. Some of the songs they are most famous for are 'Paranoid', 'Snowblind', and 'Mama, I'm Coming Home'.

Particular attention was paid to Black Sabbath by critics who were concerned with the group's fondness for imagery from religion and the black arts. This attracted much criticism, but Black Sabbath insisted that these interests reflected nothing more than theatrics. They just wanted to put on a great show. It was during this time that Ozzy started being called the 'Prince of Darkness' in the music press. But Ozzy was certainly not the only rock star to behave like a madman on stage – there were other stars such as Alice Cooper, Iggy Pop and quite a few others doing the same. In total, Ozzy stayed with Black Sabbath for ten years, but he quit the band after their Never Say Die album in 1978. Black Sabbath still lived on (with Ronnie James Dio as front-man), but the band would never be the same without him.

Ozzy, meanwhile, was eager to explore a new musical direction. With renewed ambition, Ozzy decided to go solo. He made his post-Sabbath debut in 1980 with the album titled Blizzard of Ozz, a huge commercial success, followed in 1981 by Diary of a Madman, also a multimillion seller. Ozzy's first marriage, to Thelma Mayfair, ended that same year, and on July 4, 1982, he married Sharon Arden. Their first child, Aimee Rachel, made her debut on September 2, 1983.

That Hall of Fame

Black Sabbath, one of the most influential bands in the history of rock 'n' roll, is not in the Rock and Roll Hall of Fame. No one can really explain it — some theorize that Ozzy's first group was too much of a 'kids' band', like Kiss (also not in the Hall of Fame), to pass muster with the elitist rock critics and record execs who pick nominees, or with the larger body of voters, whoever they are.

Ozzy's no stranger to this kind of contention. From the start, Black Sabbath was despised by rock critics and ignored by radio programmers, who were uncomfortable with Ozzy's use of sacred imagery. In 2000, in true Ozzy spirit, he even asked that Black Sabbath be removed from the ballot of potential inductees. 'The nomination is meaningless, because it's not voted on by the fans,' Ozzy has said. 'It's voted on by the supposed elite of the industry and the media, who've never bought an album or concert ticket in their lives, so their vote is totally irrelevant to me.' Black Sabbath and Ozzy have done just fine, selling millions and millions of records without them. And this year, the Hall is in a very embarrassing situation: it's annual ceremony is broadcast by VH1, the sister company of MTV, whose biggest star and money-maker is none other than — Ozzy Osbourne! They can't leave Black Sabbath out again, but if the band gets in after all these years, it might look like a fix. Stay tuned!

Very Heavy Stuff

Despite a lucrative solo career, life was not without some very heavy moments for Ozzy, especially in the 1980s. Fresh from the overwhelming success of his first solo album, Ozzy's brilliant twenty-six-year-old guitar player, Randy Rhoads, was killed in a tragic airplane accident in Leesburg, Florida, along with Ozzy's seamstress, Rachel Youngblood. Ozzy witnessed the horrible crash and it affected him deeply.

In 1981, an incident occurred that has haunted Ozzy's career ever since. There was this story about Ozzy biting off the head of a bat during a show. Rumour or truth? Well, put the rumour mill to rest, because according to the *Rolling Stone Encyclopedia* and other pop music references, Ozzy did in fact bite the head off a bat tossed to him by a fan at a concert in Des Moines, Iowa. The incident enraged animal lovers and, since the poor bat bit back, it resulted in a series of rabies shots for Ozzy.

'I'm not a musician,' he said to *Rolling Stone*. 'I'm a ham [show off].' This 'biting' incident, while decidedly cruel, was intended to be gripping theatre, but Ozzy had a tendency to get carried away. Fans know from the TV show that Ozzy is certainly an animal lover. A mellowed man by the early nineties, Ozzy embarked on a farewell tour.

In 1996 he began Ozzfest, an annual rockin' romp through Europe and America. The 2002 version of the tour, co-starring System of a Down, Rob Zombie, P.O.D., the Drowning Pool and many other star-level acts, began in Germany in May and ended in September in Dallas, Texas.

Daddy Dearest!

Who'd have dreamed that this once 'Prince of Darkness' would have a whole new career playing himself as a lovable dad in a weekly 'reality sit-com'? Just as any conventional father would, Ozzy frets about his daughter's dates, grows furious at the possibility that his son has been smoking in his bedroom, teases his dogs and snores on the sofa. And, believe it or not, Ozzy washes the dishes, vacuums, and takes on other household chores.

Some may refer to the gigantic success of the MTV series as an overnight sensation. It's certainly been a sensation, but for Ozzy – and for Sharon – it's been quite a journey, too.

✠ ◉ CHAPTER THREE
Sharon Osbourne, Supermum

Yes, she did have a life before she became MTV's most famous mum! Sharon Arden was born in London in the 1950s (she hesitates to say exactly which year, but some websites list it as 1952).

Her father, Don Arden, was legendary in the entertainment industry, having worked since the age of thirteen as a stand-up comic and song-and-dance man on the variety circuit. He was a brilliant mimic with a beautiful singing voice who made his name impersonating famous tenors and movie stars. Don often left his family at home while he went on tour. They lived in a nice house but, although he was talented, his income was far from steady.

Unpredictable Dad!

Sharon's parents were Jewish and spoke both Yiddish and English at home. She had one brother, David, and their mother ran the household and helped to manage Dad's unpredictable career. The family was a boisterous one. Just like her father, Sharon was known for her wild and sometimes wicked sense of humour, and a very outgoing personality. After years of living from feast to famine, Don Arden left the stage and started his own business managing other acts. Don soon earned a reputation for being tough and determined, and managed such successful acts as the Small Faces.

Sharon and her brother were teenagers at the time and obsessed with pop music.

They learned that their father's way of doing business was pretty impressive and always seemed to work. Sharon was very bright and had been a good student. After leaving school she went to work as a receptionist in her father's office. The music business had always been her passion, and her brother's, too. Don hoped to teach his children the business well enough to create a sort of Arden family dynasty. His company was managing two major acts, one of which was Electric Light Orchestra, or ELO, a synthesizer-heavy pop band; the other act was a heavy metal band known as Black Sabbath.

Ozzy Meets Sharon

Ozzy Osbourne, of course, was the lead singer of Black Sabbath, and his reputation for trouble preceded him. When Sharon first met Ozzy in her father's office, she was so terrified of him that she refused to bring a cup of tea into the room where he sat waiting for her father.

Sharon was about eighteen at the time she met Ozzy, who was then twenty-six. Ozzy was married with children, but his marriage was coming to an end. Sharon and Ozzy became friends, and she and her father worked closely with him. In 1979, when he left Black Sabbath, his problems were at an all-time high, and Ozzy feared his career was over. But Don and Sharon didn't give up on him. Don signed Ozzy as a solo performer and took over his management. Sharon introduced Ozzy to Randy Rhoads, the talented guitarist who joined Ozzy's band and worked on the album *Blizzard of Ozz*.

One day in 1981, as the *Rolling Stone Encyclopedia* reports, Sharon brought Ozzy to a meeting of Columbia Records executives who were not entirely convinced that Ozzy had what it took to be a solo star. So Sharon dreamed up a grand entrance for him, co-starring a flock of live doves. The guys in suits were impressed and Ozzy got his record deal. Sharon felt that she could do a better job of managing Ozzy's career than her father's company had done, so she asked her father to turn Ozzy's management over to her. He refused, and Sharon, who'd shrewdly stashed away over half a million pounds, proceeded to buy out her father's share of Ozzy Osbourne.

Mrs Ozzy Osbourne

Sharon and Ozzy were married on July 4, 1982, They honeymooned in Japan, where Ozzy was already a big star. They started a family and had three children in three years: Aimee, Kelly and Jack. The Osbournes also moved: from house to house, from the UK to the US and back, from the city to the country – so often, in fact, that Sharon says the family has lived in twenty-four houses in all! In spite of all the chaos – which includes being on the road with Ozzy's band for months at a time – Sharon has always provided the emotional home base for the family, no matter where they found themselves. She has also continued to manage Ozzy's career throughout all his emotional ups and downs, and the health problems that were a result of his well-chronicled battles with substance abuse.

With a staff to do the cooking and cleaning, Sharon is free to do what she does best, which is to look after her husband and kids and decorate her various houses. Her decorating style, like her mothering, can best be described as un-conventional. 'You haven't cooked for me since I was, like, seven years old,' Kelly complains to her mother in the course of one episode. 'Things are going to change around here,' Sharon replies – but what she had in mind is, so far, unclear!

Sharon in Charge

Sharon is one incredibly organised individual. She has taken over complete responsibility for just about every aspect of Ozzy's career, right down to the outfits he wears on stage. Sharon has hiring and firing power over every person involved with the rock star, and it's no surprise that throughout the industry she is viewed as a formidable businesswoman. Meanwhile, she assures her husband that all *he* needs to do is 'just be Ozzy,' – which, of course, generates an enormous amount of money for the family!

Sharon has, over the years, taken on the management of other musical acts, including the Smashing Pumpkins. When Sharon abruptly resigned from managing the indie rockers, she stated that it was for medical reasons: '[Lead singer] Billy Corgan was making me sick!' she shouted to the world.

The Tiger

It is this inimitable outspoken style that has earned Sharon her reputation as someone who gets what she wants, and usually on her own terms – just like her father. She is very protective of her children, and has been compared to a mother tiger protecting her cubs. She defends them fiercely against any outside attacks and does so in her own irreverent way. When their noisy neighbours were getting out of hand, Sharon tried to reason with them, and even invited them in for a cup of tea. But when threatened by them, she didn't shy away. She's a brilliant negotiator for her family's good. What a mum!

Sharon's Deal of the Century

The Osbournes is clearly the crown jewel in Sharon's tiara. She brought the show to MTV (inspired in part by an episode of *Cribs* the children did a year before), and within a few weeks of its first transmission theirs was the most-watched show in MTV's history, garnering rave reviews from critics. The show was a sensation!

After the Osbourne family's wildly successful first season on the air, MTV asked the family to consider a second season. According to trade papers, Sharon negotiated a multimillion-dollar contract, which included various unusual demands such as psychotherapy for all of the Osbournes' household pets. That's just another example of her instinct for show business flair, something she has in common with Ozzy. Sharon did finally agree to sign the contract, but in the outrageous theatrical style that has become her trademark, and in true heavy metal fashion, she jokingly offered to sign it in blood! The news came hand in hand with the announcement that Kelly would be making her singing debut on the 2002 MTV Movie Awards show.

Grooving to the Music

Sharon's taste is eclectic. She wears casual over-sized T-shirts and capris around the house, then steps out in a stunning pink Chanel suit to visit royalty. She listens to everything from Led Zeppelin to Pavarotti. Of course she loves Black Sabbath, but she also loves Vivaldi's Four Seasons. For the record, when she's on her own, listening to music in her car or at the house with no one around, her favourite band of all is Queen. As far as new bands go, Sharon says Jack forces her to listen to Tool, but she likes Foo Fighters and Coldplay. In her opinion, a lot of the so-called new young bands are doing something retro, something she's seen and heard before in her many years in the music business as both manager and fan. But she's always looking for something she thinks is really new, so she goes out regularly to hear bands play in Los Angeles.

Supermum!

Sharon attends lots of musical events in her roles as wife and manager of the 'Prince of Darkness' and mother of the Osbourne kids, and she's a glamorous celebrity in her own right. But given the choice of attending star-studded parties all over the world or staying home, Sharon says she prefers a quiet night in!

But does she ever relax? Her family says no, never. Ozzy lovingly says Sharon is a lunatic workaholic who works day and night. Sharon says she only sleeps about four to five hours a night because she has to get up early to make phone calls to Europe and to get the kids out of bed. She has an office, although it doesn't look like a typical one. Sometimes it's in her home or in the carriage house in the grounds.

Sharon loves making deals, but most of all she loves her family. She has managed to find a unique way to make it all work for her, so that she can do what she loves *and* spend time with the people she loves.

Sharon's Biggest Battle

Some might consider just being Mrs Ozzy Osbourne a major trial in itself. But for Sharon, even through the ups and downs of Ozzy's alcohol and substance abuse, love has conquered all. During their years together Sharon has been Ozzy's wife, confidant, best friend, playmate and business partner. She is always there to smooth over the hazards that come their way.

On July 1, 2002, straight after the first season of MTV's *The Osbournes* wrapped, Sharon was diagnosed with cancer of the colon. If Sharon was shaken, Ozzy almost went to pieces, and was immediately at her side. The night before her surgery, the two stayed up all night holding and comforting each other.

Ozzy explains: 'She's my soulmate . . . She's my whole world . . . She has been my pillar of strength for many years.' The news of Sharon's illness marked a turning point. Ozzy had to be the strong one – especially when post-surgery tests showed that the cancer had spread and Sharon was going to have to undergo three months of chemotherapy. In typical Sharon style she took it in her stride, saying, 'I always knew how precious and lucky it is to be alive, and now even more so. I have a million more things I'm going to do. And I'm not going anywhere.'

Now *that's* a Supermum!

✠ CHAPTER FOUR
Princess Kelly

Ozzy and Sharon's second child, Kelly, was born here in the UK on October 27, 1984 – eighteen months after her older sister, Aimee, and just thirteen months before the birth of her brother, Jack. So for a while there were three adorable toddlers in the Osbourne household.

Schooling

Kelly has attended both state and private schools, and has had homeschooling from tutors. Like her brother, Jack, she has struggled with the reading problem dyslexia. What's more, she's often been taken out of school to travel on the road with her father's band – so her education has been an unusual one. Kelly has always had a nanny (named Melinda), who's sort of a personal family assistant, to keep things running as smoothly as possible. Luckily for Kelly, she also has a loving family and faithful friends who are around to listen to her problems and opinions – and Kelly seems to have an opinion on just about everything.

An Original

There's never been another teenage character on television, live or scripted, who looks or talks like Kelly Osbourne. She hangs out at the house with the TV cameras rolling, wearing no make up, in her rolled-waistband sweatpants, her hair in electro-shock mode, while she chews her nails, complains, laughs and whines without a trace of self-consciousness. She'll bop brother Jack over the head, or snuggle up to her father, Ozzy, and plant a kiss on his forehead in front of a delighted camera crew. What a girl!

Unlike most girls her age, Kelly doesn't seem to be obsessed with her looks or her weight. While young people are bombarded by messages that they have to look a certain way, Kelly is refreshing and confident and refuses to worry about her weight. She told *The Times*, 'My physique goes against everything L.A. stands for.' Continuing to explain the reason for her remarkable self-confidence, she added: 'I've got my dad's gift for making a fool of myself in public and not caring, and my mum's sense of humour and strength. I guess that's it.'

And that is pretty cool! Some viewers think that Kelly is the only sane member of her famous family. For all her flamboyant fashions, pink hair and colourful language, Kelly is, after all, a pretty well-adjusted, likeable teen, with many of the same problems faced by other girls her age: her brother gets on her nerves, her parents often embarrass her, and she hates maths. Nothing so unusual there!

Kelly on the Town

Although Kelly lives in a beautiful house, she likes to socialize and get out around town. After she has done her homework, Kelly will hit some Los Angeles hot spots, like the famous rock star mecca the Roxy or the outrageous Standard Hotel. Even surrounded by other celebrities, or the children of celebrities, Kelly stands out. When she walks into a room, she stops traffic. But she's got used to that, and soon gets into mingling and mixing just like everybody else.

Kelly's been heard to complain about people in or around her crowd who are rude and pretentious. She likes to think that, unlike many other rich kids, she is not obsessed with money or fashion — although the family money certainly allows her to maintain a fabulous lifestyle. Kelly's passions are shopping, hanging out, and listening to music. She also enjoys being on TV, and though she might roll her eyes at her family's kooky antics, she really adores her parents and her brother. Kelly said in an interview that her mother is so cool that, if Sharon were eighteen, Kelly would want to hang out with her. And that's a compliment any mum would appreciate!

The Pink Suite

Kelly has two whole rooms to herself — a bedroom plus a sitting room with a sleepover couch. Everything in her bedroom is pink, Kelly's signature colour. She also has two bathrooms, one for herself and one for guests, because she doesn't like other people using her stuff. She retreats to her room when her family and the cameras get a bit too much for her.

She rearranges the furniture often and changes her collection of chairs the way some people change their shoes. When she sees a new one that she likes better than one she already has, in comes the new and out goes the old! Although she never has enough people over to sit in all her chairs, she can't stop buying more. One of her favourites is from the set of the famous movie *A Clockwork Orange*. She also has a great bubble chair that hangs from the ceiling.

The Music in Her Life

When a reporter asked Kelly what her favourite CD of all time was, she slyly answered that she couldn't say because she hasn't lived long enough to tell! Give her another twenty years, she added, and ask again. But Kelly's been surrounded by music all her life, so in spite of her saying this, it's clear that she *does* know what she likes and what she doesn't. At home, Kelly likes to mix old music and new. She'll listen to the White Stripes, then switch to the best of Blondie from the late seventies, or the pioneering Velvet Underground, a sixties group discovered by the famous artist Andy Warhol. She listens to the Strokes and Starsailor, but loves old-timers like Madonna, whose hit single 'Papa Don't Preach' was Kelly's own first hit song and the one with which she made her MTV debut. It shot straight into the US top ten and, as we go to press, is anticipated to do the same in the UK. One thing Kelly doesn't like is being blasted by Jack's favourite new metal bands when they're playing through speakers all over the house and there's no place to escape.

Dad Ozzy is certainly one performer who Kelly's heard lots of during her life. Where some families picnic or go boating together, the Osbournes stage a rock tour and bring everyone along! Kelly's favourite Ozzy songs are 'Paranoid' from *Live Evil* and 'Crazy Train' from *We Sold Our Soul for Rock and Roll.*

It's no surprise that Kelly is an eager concert-goer. She told *Interview* magazine that she's seen the band Incubus 'about 35,000 times.' Now that's a fan!

Kelly's Style

During an Internet chat session Kelly was asked if she preferred punk fashion, fifties vintage, or sporty casual style. She answered: 'I like the eighties. I'm a little eighties girl. And I've always wanted to design clothes, so later on I may do that.'

Kelly is more of a trendsetter than a follower of fashion and always manages to put together her own original look. She told MTV that she doesn't like putting together outfits totally designed by someone else and she doesn't buy into anyone else's idea of how you should look. 'I live in L.A.,' she said, 'surrounded by tall, skinny blondes, which I'll obviously never be, so I've got to work with what I've got.'

With her fashion inspirations being Cyndi Lauper and Madonna, Kelly borrows from a wide spectrum of styles and designers. Some of her favourite designers are British original Zandra Rhodes and German minimalist Helmut Lang. She likes bags by Bloom and lots of things from Dolce & Gabbana, Versus and Diesel. Among her favourite stores are Barney's and Fred Segal in Los Angeles.

That Hair!

The shade worn by Kelly during her first season on MTV is called Pink Flamingo, from Fudge.

She had to take some colour out of her naturally light hair to get that vibrant pink, so she uses lots of conditioner to keep her hair soft. It's a lot of work, in fact, to keep her hair bright, shiny – and healthy, too! She'll apply Kiehl's Silk Groom for condition and a hot oil treatment to keep her scalp healthy. Her spikes are courtesy of Bed Head wax sticks. As she told MTV, 'I don't really care what people think about my hair. It's my hair, so why should they care? Ooh, that rhymed!'

Skincare and Make-up

Kelly pampers her skin with a good cleansing ritual and has found that Shiseido facial cleansers work well for her. Like any teenager she gets spots and she tackles these with some Sisley facial pads and MAC toners. When it comes to make-up, like her dad, Kelly likes MAC's eyeliner.

When she's pulling all the stops out she'll use a lot of eyeliner and some MAC eye shadow, too. She outlines her mouth with a little lip liner, then fills in with Chanel Infrarouge Whisperlight. A favourite product is Chanel's Crayon Visage Duo Face Colour Pencil, because it works on eyes, lips and cheeks, which is pretty handy when you have to 'do your face' in the back of a limo!

Tattoo

As viewers now know, Kelly has a tattoo of a heart on her hip. She says getting it was a bit of an annoying pain, but that it didn't really hurt – she just wanted to get it over with. She was also afraid that her mum would hit the roof! So she made Ozzy (a walking tattoo museum) tell Sharon, who was upset for a bit, but soon got over it.

Can Kelly Do Just About Anything She Wants?

Kelly says she has a lot of freedom because her parents trust her. She told *Interview* magazine, 'My parents don't really worry about me because I'm not like the other kids. I'm not easily influenced to do things. I do what I want to and am prepared to pay the consequences.'

So Kelly's formula for freedom is: earn your parents' trust and show them that you're not going to dumbly succumb to peer pressure. Show them you're responsible, and they'll let you do more.

Like everyone else, Kelly doesn't like curfews, but she knows that a phone call, if she's going to be late, is better than having worried parents and a scene when she does get home. Kelly appreciates that if she wants to pursue her dream of a career in music, she has to be responsible, do her homework, show up on time, and get along with others, although it may some-times be a struggle. But where can any girl learn more about being herself and getting along with others than in the amazing Osbourne household?

✠ CHAPTER FIVE
Jack Sabbath Osbourne, Young Man on the Move

Born November 8, 1985, Jack Sabbath Osbourne was named after his dad Ozzy's band. Although Jack isn't keen on being asked what it's like to be Ozzy's son, Jack Sabbath is a fitting name for this precocious teenager who has been immersed in heavy metal music since he was a baby.

'My Little Man'

Before he could even walk, Jack accompanied his dad on his tours around America and the rest of

The Osbournes – featuring Ozzy, Sharon, Kelly and Jack –
is the biggest hit in MTV history.

Osbournes then …
(L. to R.) Jack, Sharon, Kelly, first-born Aimee and Ozzy.

Osbournes now…
Sharon, Kelly, Ozzy, Aimee and Jack.

Mama don't preach – Kelly and Sharon share a love of shopping and pets. This is their dog Minnie.

Jack has become a talent scout for
up-and-coming rock bands.

A fan poses in front of the most famous house
on the block, Casa Osbourne!

'It's weird. I don't think me or Jack ever thought for a day in our life that this sort of thing would happen to us.' – Kelly

'I think we've all pretty much handled it [fame] the same. My kids are doing a pretty good job handling it.' – Ozzy

'I'm a mum and this is the kids – and he's the rock star,' says Sharon. She makes it sound easy!

Kelly's 'star' is on the rise – and glittering!

The Osbournes are all about family.

'I love you more than life itself ... but you're all mad.' – Ozzy

the world. Ozzy would often bring Jack on stage with him and introduce him to his fans. Dad even dedicated his song 'My Little Man' to Jack. Although at 5'8" he's not so little anymore, Jack is still his father's 'little man.' What's more, his unique education is already paying off as Jack carves out his own place in the world of rock 'n' roll.

When he's not out on tour, a typical day for Jack begins at nine a.m. when Melinda begins to try and wake him. His homeschooling is supposed to begin at ten, but Jack will be the first to tell you that a teenager's brain isn't functional until ten-thirty. Like his dad, Jack suffers from dyslexia and attention deficit disorder. Before he had a home tutor, Jack attended a special school for dyslexic kids.

After his studies, Jack works out in the home gym before heading to his job (three days a week) as a talent scout for Epic Records. His years of touring with Ozzy have given him an excellent ear for discovering new bands. One band he found already has a development deal at Epic.

'It's a Good Time'

After a hard day's work, Jack likes to play just as hard. One of Jack's favourite sayings is 'It's a good time.' As he wrote on his MTV online diary, that's 'anything that is fun, cool, or exciting.' Jack loves playing the drums and is hoping for a soundproof booth to be put in the house so he can practise without adding to the already considerable noise of the Osbourne home. His beloved dog is Lola, who he loves to wrestle and swim in the pool with. Just don't ask him to clean up after her! Going out to rock clubs like the Roxy, the Viper Room and the Whiskey-a-Go-Go on Los Angeles's Sunset Strip is also 'a good time' for Jack, as well as an opportunity for him to spot hot new bands. Jack also likes to hang out with friends in his room. They'll stay up late listening to music, talking or watching a movie.

Chez Jack

A personal sanctuary and bachelor pad, Jack's room says a lot about who he is. Decorated in dark, masculine colours, it's full of high-tech equipment. He has a TV, VCR and DVD ('the best invention ever') with surround-sound and, naturally, tons of CDs. He's got a major book collection, too, which includes a first edition of the Tolkien classic *The Lord of the Rings*.

Jack shares his dad's love of skulls, mixing them with other prized possessions such as a guitar, trophies and a Chef doll from South Park. A prominent place on his shelves is reserved for an Osbourne family portrait.

In complete contrast, Jack's bathroom is very white and bright – the perfect place to showcase his toothbrush collection. 'I don't really know why I have so many toothbrushes,' he says on one all-Jack website. 'It's a good time, though: one for every day of the week.'

The youngest Osbourne keeps a small and tight-knit circle of friends around him. He says it's hard as the kid of a celebrity (or now, as a celebrity himself) to know who your real friends are – so many are just attracted to the money and glamorous lifestyle. He told MTV: 'What makes a good friend is when they start caring – when you're sick and they actually call you and see how you're doing.' Jack doesn't have a girlfriend at the moment, but he loves to open up his room to his friends. Sometimes friends can become a bit *too* comfortable: Jason Dill, one of Jack's best mates, practically moved in – much to Ozzy and Sharon's annoyance!

On Jack's Shelves

A few of the artists found in Jack's CD collection:

Coldplay
Faith No More
Hatebreed
Incubus
Nebula
Nirvana
Primus
Queens of the Stone Age
Radiohead
Rage Against the Machine
Rob Zombie
Slipknot
Tool (Aenima, *his all-time favourite*)
Ugly Kid Joe

Jack in Black

When it comes to fashion, Jack likes to keep it simple. His favourite colour is black and he rarely wears anything else. 'I wore black Dickies [basic work trousers] for two years straight,' he told MTV. 'I kind of do my own thing.' Jack's 'nerdy' glasses are also a trademark of his style. He's become more adventurous in recent months, trading in his curly brown hair for various new styles and colours. After all, as Jack said to one hopeful band seeking a label, 'You've gotta have good hair to get a deal in development.'

Jackfest

When Jack was younger, the annual Ozzfest used to be like summer camp for him. Gradually, though, as Jack has learned more and more about the family business, he has also taken on more responsibility – by 2002 he had eighty-five percent of the say of who performed on the Second Stage. A showcase for up-and-coming acts, it's the perfect venue for Jack to develop new bands. With Ozzy claiming that this will be his final year headlining the heavy metal festival, Jack may well be running it in a few years' time.

2002 Ozzfest Second Stage Lineup

Check out some of the bands Jack invited to be part of his dad's high-profile tour:

☆ Andrew W.K.   ☆ Mushroomhead

☆ Chevelle   ☆ Neurotica

☆ Down   ☆ Otep

☆ Flaw   ☆ Pulse Ultra

☆ Glassjaw   ☆ Seether

☆ Hatebreed   ☆ Soil

✠ CHAPTER SIX
What Kind of Parents are Sharon and Ozzy?

Ozzy and Sharon Osbourne's kids stay out until all hours, come and go as they please, dye their hair crayon colours, get themselves tattooed and curse like a rock 'n' roll road crew. What do Sharon and Ozzy do about all this?

Not much, it would seem. They appear to enforce very few of the rules that are standard in most households. As a matter of fact, they indulge in some of these same antics. They swear just as much as their kids, if not more, dye their hair unnatural colours, get tattoos (Ozzy, at least) and engage in what would normally be considered fairly antisocial behaviour. So what kind of parents are they, anyway? Let's take a look at some of their parenting techniques.

Papa Does Preach

Ozzy doesn't exactly lecture his kids in the usual way. He does, however, talk to them very frankly about all the big topics parents are supposed to warn their kids about but don't always know how to handle: the dangers of sex, drugs, smoking and drinking.

Ozzy's style with this is pretty straight-forward. Having quit smoking cigarettes after more than forty years, he disapproves of smoking of any kind and absolutely forbids it in the house. He tells his kids that if they really want to be unique they shouldn't get any tattoos, because everyone already has them. He also warns them not to get caught drinking or taking drugs – not least because, as guests of the US, they could be deported. He wants to avoid being hypocritical, given his well-known lifelong battles with addiction. But because of his own many outrageous excesses, he tries to give his children the benefit of his experience. Ozzy knows this can be tough. He says, 'I think being a parent is the most difficult job on the face of the earth. You hate to say things that will upset your kids, but then sometimes you have to because you can't let them run around wild.'

She's Heavy. She's Our Mother.

Sharon's the one entrusted with the role of the 'heavy' more often than Ozzy. She's the one who insists on the kids having a curfew, because she's the one who can't get to sleep unless they're safe at home. Compared to other kids, however, their curfew is exceptionally reasonable (midnight during the week and two-thirty a.m. on weekends) and can be extended with a well-timed phone call under the right circumstances. As she told MTV in an interview last spring: 'I try to treat them as young adults and hope they'll give me back the respect, so if they want to stay out later than curfew then they're not afraid of picking up the phone to say, "Look, this is what's going on, this is where I want to go, can I go?" Instead of, like, being afraid to pick up the phone and call.' This method seems to work pretty effectively – although it is usually Kelly who ends up calling on her and Jack's behalf to get a curfew extension. At least Sharon knows where they are, that they're all right, and when she can expect them home. Kelly and Jack know that she cares about them and that if they come home later than agreed upon they are robbing their busy mother of her sleep – and there will be a price to pay. They'd usually rather avoid a flare-up from Sharon.

No Secrets

Sharon and Ozzy talk to Kelly and Jack about everything – the care of the dogs, the working of the vacuum cleaner, the outfit Ozzy's wearing for a show. Sharon also talks extensively, especially with Kelly, about matters of romance. Sharon shared her views on the 'birds and the bees' with MTV: 'As much as you think you love someone, it's puppy love, it's infatuation, and you've got to take your time. I try to make [her] realize how special [she is] just by being a woman. All women are special.' Sharon tries to teach Jack to be responsible and to treat women respectfully. She says, 'Sure, there's tons of girls that want to go with Jack because of who [he] is. What I try to tell Jack is to just have respect for that woman because she's a woman like your mum, like your sisters.'

Ozzy and Sharon have high expectations of their kids, but these don't include getting A's at school, or getting into university or becoming an Olympic athlete. They simply expect their kids to do their best at everything they do and to treat people well. Ozzy understands that school has been difficult for his kids, like it was for him. But he says, 'Education's come a long way, and Sharon's done a remarkable job.' Sharon's views on schoolwork are very clear. She understands that her children have learning disabilities, but she doesn't let them use that as an excuse to be lazy. She has said that she doesn't mind their failing a test as long as they've studied and done their best. Sharon tells Kelly and Jack that it's a waste of their time and everyone else's if they don't try at school.

Room to Grow

Kelly and Jack are so close in age and have spent so much time together that they should have had a lot of practice in getting along with each other. But in fact they often drive each other crazy. Their sibling rivalries are sometimes so intense that they disrupt the entire household. At times their parents do intervene, but often they back off to allow Kelly and Jack to work it out themselves.

Like many teenagers, Kelly has a tendency to temper tantrums, or prolonged whining and sulking sessions, which Ozzy has dubbed her 'wobblers.' By referring to these freakouts in this way, Ozzy has actually come up with an ingenious technique. He recognizes and validates Kelly's irrational behaviour by giving it a special name, yet at the same time he defuses some of her anger by giving it a humorous spin. How long would you be able to stay mad when you're having another 'wobbler'? When it comes to parenting, Ozzy is at times more savvy than he admits.

All They Need Is Love

Most importantly, Kelly and Jack and Sharon and Ozzy quite obviously love one another very much. Ozzy says that he would do anything to make his wife and kids happy. He told *Interview* magazine, 'I love my dogs, my kids, my wife, my house. I loved my wife before the [MTV] show and I love her now. To see my wife and children happy, that's all that matters to me.'

He and Sharon involve their children in almost every aspect of their work and lives and encourage them to follow their own dreams. Kelly wants to sing – her parents help her make it happen. Jack wants to have his own record label – they get him started and guide him. Ozzy and Sharon accept Kelly and Jack exactly as they are and show their children that they are important to them and that they are supportive of their talents. Meanwhile, they have a lot of laughs. What kind of parents do they sound like to *you*?

✠ CHAPTER SEVEN
The Extended Family

The Osbournes have an extended circle of family and friends who are very important to them. Take a look at some of the people who share their lives:

✠Family

Ozzy has three children from his first marriage, to Thelma Mayfair. He adopted the son she already had, Elliot Kingsley, when he was five years old. Ozzy and Thelma then had two other children.

Jessica Starshine Osbourne is Ozzy's oldest child and likes to keep a low profile. Jess is almost thirty, and she's so shy that she usually just goes by Jessica Starshine to avoid letting people know that her dad is the famous musician.

Louis Jon Osbourne lives in England and is a well-known techno DJ. He's twenty-seven and has his own website. He has a good sense of humour, and Sharon says he's 'a big part of the family.'

Aimee Rachel Osbourne is Sharon and Ozzy's oldest child. Like her father and sister she's a singer and musician, but she's not famous – yet! She chose to keep a low profile during the filming of the show, but she does appear in a couple of the episodes – only they blur her face out. She may appear in a couple of episodes of the second season on MTV, so maybe we'll get to hear some of her music, too.

✠Friends

The Woods have known the Osbournes for a while. Elijah Wood (the actor who played Frodo in *The Lord of the Rings*) and his sister, Hannah, both show up at the house from time to time. Elijah even helps clean up some dog mess in one episode – now *that's* a friend!

Robert is Kelly's 'best friend' and not her boyfriend – although he sure is around a lot! The verdict is still out on that one. She obviously adores him, and he went to a lot of trouble to buy her a birthday gift she'd really like.

Michael is the Osbournes' security guard, hired to watch the house. Besides walking the grounds and protecting their home, Michael likes playing pool. Once, he was mistakenly arrested when neighbours thought he was an intruder at the house!

Melinda Varga She's the Osbournes' nanny and as such she is definitely a big part of the family, despite not being related by blood. She's married and comes from Melbourne, Australia. Melinda helps the family out in many ways beyond her duties – although she tries to avoid getting too wrapped up all in their crazy dramas and arguments! When things get too chaotic, she puts on her headphones and listens to her favourite music.

Jason Dill is the pro skater who overstayed his welcome at the Osbourne house. He annoyed Ozzy with his constant head-scratching and made Sharon a little angry when he melted a plastic chicken on her stove and didn't even help clean it up! (Yuck!)

Giacomo Osbourne?

'I'm Ozzy Osbourne,' the man born John Michael Osbourne says at the end of the first season. 'It could be worse . . . I could be Sting.' It could be a lot worse for Jack and Kelly, too, had their parents followed the trend of kid-naming among other rock stars.

Here are a few examples of some rock stars and their unusually named children:

Bono	Elijah Bob Patricius Guggi Q Memphis Eve
David Bowie	Duncan Zowie
Cher	Elijah Blue Chastity

Kurt Cobain	Frances Bean
Alice Cooper	Calico
Bob Geldof	Fifi Trixibelle
	Peaches Honeyblossom
	Pixie
Michael Hutchence	Heavenly Hirani
	Tiger Lily
Michael Jackson	Prince Michael
	Jackson, Jr.
	Paris Michael
	Katherine Jackson
Madonna	Lourdes
	Rocco
Sting	Giacomo

The Osbourne Zoo

Not all of the members of the extended Osbourne family walk on two legs. In fact, most of them use four!

The Osbournes have seven dogs and two cats. Their most famous dogs are Lola, the bulldog who practically gets an entire episode to herself (for pooping in the corner!), and Pipi, a black Pomeranian who got lost for a month but was finally returned. The other dogs are two Japanese Chins named Maggie and New Baby, another Pomeranian named Minnie, a Chihuahua who goes by the name of Martin, and Ozzy's favourite, Lulu. And let's not forget the two cats, Puss and GusGus.

Despite having all these animals in their home, the Osbournes aren't necessarily that good at controlling them. Housetraining Lola, for example, seemed an insurmountable challenge. To combat this the family called in a dog therapist called Tamara, who claimed to be making great progress with their most troublesome pet – moments before she made yet another puddle on the expensive rug!

✠ CHAPTER EIGHT
Osbourne Astrology

Ozzy: December 3, 1948

It would be an understatement to say that Ozzy is an unconventional dad. That may be because he's the classic sign of a rock star: Sagittarius. Sagittarians love travelling, which is perfect for someone who has lived all over the world and spends part of every year on tour. Also, Sagittarians are almost never shy and retiring — which is why Ozzy's such a great performer.

Sharon: who Knows?

Sharon is notoriously tight-lipped about her birthday, but judging by her zany, wild take on life, she could be an Aries. This fits in perfectly with Ozzy; since they're both Fire signs, they understand each other.

Kelly: October 27, 1984
Jack: November 8, 1985

Jack and Kelly are both Scorpios. This has a lot to do with why they're unfazed by having the 'Prince of Darkness' as a father (unlike their older sister, Aimee, who's a Virgo and much more coy about who her dad is). This also explains why they fight constantly: scorpios rarely like sharing territory. Still, underneath it all, you can tell they love each other dearly.

How Would You Fit into the Osbourne Family?

Although you and Sharon might butt heads every once in a while, you'd understand: she's just being a mum. You'd probably try to stay out of the constant bickering that Jack and Kelly seem to revel in, but they'd both try to get you on their side, because you're so strong-minded!

Unlike Jack and Kelly, who are often a little rude to the Osbourne nanny, Melinda, you'd know how to be nice to her. As a result, you could be sure she'd always stick up for you, no matter what – even when it really was you who threw a bagel in the neighbour's yard. Plus, you'd be good to have around, because you'd never forget important stuff, like feeding the many dogs or letting them out so they could stop doing their business in the house!

This family could sure benefit from your ability to put yourself in someone else's shoes. All those people who get into spats with the Osbournes, like those rude neighbours, would appreciate your perspective on things. Maybe you could even get Ozzy to stop throwing firewood through people's windows! And when one of Jack's friends overstayed his welcome, you'd be good at letting them know without hurting their feelings.

You'd be as thick as thieves with either Kelly or Jack (but probably not both, since they fight so much). Cancers are super-sensitive, so you'd be able to tell how much you could get away with and when it's time to call it quits. Everyone in this family could benefit from your kindness and practical skills. If you know how to make a grilled cheese sandwich or pop popcorn, you'd be a treasured asset.

★ LEO ★

Jul 24 - Aug 23

Another ambitious superstar in the making! Luckily for you, it seems the Osbourne family's spotlight is always wide and bright enough so that everyone gets a chance to shine. And you can be sure that everyone would do their best to support you in whatever you decided to do: just look at how much energy they all put into Kelly's musical career! Meanwhile, you'd be a great friend to have cheering along backstage when each of the other Osbournes was taking their turn in the spotlight. Your warmth, enthusiasm and generous nature would blend brilliantly with the rest of the family.

If you lived in this family, they certainly wouldn't need to hire trainers for their dogs and cats. Before long, the Osbourne zoo would be following you around, and there wouldn't be any more embarrassing accidents in the house, that's for sure. You'd save the Osbournes a fortune on pet therapists. Although you might occasionally get annoyed about having your life captured on film, you'd probably get used to it and even learn how to have fun, in spite of the camera crews.

The Osbournes have a very individualistic style. But you could definitely lend a little class to their house. Although you might be embarrassed when they start blasting Black Sabbath out of the windows, you'd be there to smooth things over. And none of your friends would overstay their welcome!

77

Just what this family needs, another Scorpio! Scorpios often need a lot of space, because they're very individualistic people. You like having privacy and room to grow. Ultimately, you'd do fine with these guys, as long as you had your own bedroom and bathroom. Although there'd definitely be run-ins with the other Scorpios in the house, Jack and Kelly, you'd also have the benefit of really understanding each other. How many brothers and sisters can say that?

Although you and Ozzy would be different in almost every way (let's face it: there's no one quite like him, is there?), the benefit of being the same star sign would mean that you'd always understand him, even when he's being really mumbly and weird. You could act as a translator for the rest of the family – which could really come in handy those times when no one seems to know what Ozzy's talking about.

You'd be pretty angry whenever Jack woke you in the middle of the night with his heavy metal music. But most of the time you'd feel lucky to live in such an exciting family. Usually you'd probably just shake your head and laugh at all their ridiculous antics, but every once in a while you might try to talk some sense into them. And if that didn't work, you'd probably just throw up your hands and join in!

Maybe the Osbournes are lucky that you're not in their family: with a mind as creative as yours around, who knows what kind of trouble they'd get into? Also, since you're so good at keeping secrets, you'd be in a lot of the family's plots. Kelly would take you with her to get a tattoo, or maybe Jack would share his CD collection with you.

Some people might think you tender Pisceans would be too sensitive for a house as wild and rude as the Osbournes'. But you'd actually be perfect for it, because Pisceans are the most adaptable of all signs. Although you might be reluctant to scream at the slightest provocation while the rest of the family do, it probably wouldn't faze you too much, either. And having your kind presence around would always be a good way for people to soothe their frayed nerves.

✠ CHAPTER NINE
What's Your Ozz-Q?

A tricky test of your knowledge of obscure Osbourne lore . . .

1) Jack's bulldog Lola is named after

   a) Lola Falana

   b) Madonna's daughter, Lourdes

   c) Gina Lollabrigida

   d) The title of a classic Kinks song

2) Which dish can every member of the Osbourne family prepare?

   a) Steven Tyler's 'Trout Meunière'

b) Humble pie

c) Alpo

d) Microwave popcorn

3) For which very famous celebrity did Ozzy have the honour to perform in June 2002?

a) Queen Elizabeth II

b) The Pope

c) Mike Tyson

d) Liza Minnelli

4) Ozzy's favourite musician is

a) Beethoven

b) Stevie Wonder

c) Paul McCartney

d) Posh Spice

5) Ozzy told which celebrity that he was happy the celebrity got out of his recent legal troubles?

a) Bo Diddley

b) Sean Combs

c) Sean John

d) Puff Daddy

6) **Which celebrity did Ozzy take photos with in episode three?**

a) P. Diddy

b) Dee Dee Ramone

c) Puffy

d) Buffy St. Marie

7) **Which famous team composed some of the musical shows that Ozzy appeared in as a child?**

a) Gilbert and Sullivan

b) Dolce & Gabbana

c) Marks and Spencer

d) Simon and Garfunkel

8) **Which famous prince jumped up and down during a recent performance of Ozzy's in London?**
   a) Freddy Prinze, Jr.
   b) The Artist Formerly Known As Prince
   c) Prince William
   d) The Prince of Darkness

9) **In the outfit Ozzy wears for the video in episode five, he looks most like:**
   a) Dame Edna Everage
   b) Lorna Luft
   c) Scarlett O'Hara
   d) Christina Aguilera

10) **Which of the following bands was on Jack's Second Stage in the 2002 Ozzfest?**
   a) The Carpenters
   b) Meshuggah
   c) Deep Purple
   d) 'N Sync

Answers:

1d; 2c; 3a; 4c; 5b, c, or d; 6a; 7a; 8c; 9d; 10b.

Give yourself five points for each correct answer and a bonus of ten if you picked all three correct answers to number five!

✠ How'd you do?

65: You still need this book, maybe more than ever!

51-64: Go back and think seriously about the ones you missed!

36-50: Go back and spend some more quality time in front of your TV!

25-35: You probably made some lucky guesses.

0-24: Brain rot becomes you!

✠ CHAPTER TEN
Facts 'n' Stats

✠ Ozzy's Basics

Real name: John Michael Osbourne

Nicknames: Ozzy, Prince of Darkness

Birthday: December 3, 1948

Star sign: Sagittarius

Birthplace: Birmingham

Childhood residence: 14 Lodge Road, Aston, Birmingham

Current British residence: A hundred-year-old farmhouse called Welders House in Buckinghamshire, about 40 minutes from London

Current U.S. residence: A Spanish-style mansion in Beverly Hills, California

Height: 5' 10"

Weight: 160 lbs

Parents: John and Lillian Osbourne (John was a tool maker and Lillian worked in a car factory)

Siblings: Paul, Tony, Jean, Iris and Gillian

Wife: Sharon Osbourne

Children: Elliot, Jessica Starshine, Louis, Aimee, Kelly and Jack

Wedding to Sharon: In Maui, Hawaii on July 4, 1982

Honeymoon with Sharon: Japan

Instrument: Harmonica

OZZY'S FAVES

COLOUR: Black

BAND: The Beatles

MUSICIAN: Paul McCartney

MORE OF OZZY'S FAVES

NEIGHBOUR: 1950s–1960s teen idol singer Pat Boone – Ozzy says, 'You may say that Pat Boone is a nerd, but he was a great neighbour.'

ARTWORK: Skulls and crosses – there are hundreds of them in the Osbourne house

TV WATCHING PARTNER: Michael, the family security guard

TV CHANNEL: The History Channel

COFFEE: French vanilla-flavoured Cremora

SOFT DRINK: Diet Coke

SKIN CLEANSER: Osea's Ocean Cleansing Mudd

COLOGNE: Czech & Speake No. 88

ROOM IN THE OSOURNE HOUSE: The kitchen

SUNGLASSES: Lunor 1 makes his signature blue shade

✠ Sharon's Basics

Real name: Sharon Arden Osbourne
Birthday: Rumoured to be 1952
Star sign: Possibly Aries
Birthplace: London
Current US residence: Beverly Hills, California
Height: 5' 2"
Parents: Don and Hope Arden
Siblings: David
Husband: Ozzy Osbourne
Children: Aimee, Kelly and Jack
Dogs: 2 Pomeranians, Minnie and Pipi; 2 Japanese Chins, Maggie and New Baby; 2 Chihuahuas, Martin and Lulu; bulldog, Lola; cats, Puss and GusGus
Job: Music manager – she has been Ozzy's manager since 1982 (she has also managed Smashing Pumpkins, Lita Ford, Coal Chamber, Quireboys, Gary Moore)

SHARON'S FAVES

COLOUR: Black

BANDS: All-time favourite — Queen; but also Black Sabbath, Led Zeppelin (Sharon also loves classical music)

CLASSICAL SINGER: Pavarotti

CLASSICAL COMPOSITION: Vivaldi's Four Seasons

SONG: John Lennon's Imagine — it was Sharon and Ozzy's favourite song when they were dating and first fell in love.

CURRENT BANDS: Coldplay, Foo Fighters

FOODS: French fries, milk shakes and ice cream — even though she had a stomach banding operation for weight reduction in 1999. 'I just eat little bits', she says.

SKINCARE PRODUCTS: Sisley

PASTIME: Shopping

✠ Aimee's Basics

Real name: Aimee Rachel Osbourne

Birthday: September 2, 1983

Star sign: Virgo

Birthplace: England

Parents: Ozzy and Sharon Osbourne

Siblings: Kelly and Jack

Career goal: A career in music

Surprise move: Aimee declined to be part of the first season of MTV's *The Osbournes*, and during the six months of filming she moved into the family's guesthouse. Don't be surprised if she shows up in the second season.

Sharon's description: 'I think Aimee [is] the normal one in the family.'

Fashion style: According to Kelly, Aimee is 'preppy' – khaki pants and two-piece cardigan set and loafers.

✠ Kelly's Basics

Real name: Kelly Lee Osbourne

Birthday: October 27, 1984

Star sign: Scorpio

Birthplace: England

Current US residence: Beverly Hills, California

Parents: Ozzy and Sharon Osbourne

Siblings: Aimee and Jack

Tattoo: A small pink heart on her left hip

Celebrity best friend: Singer/actress Mandy Moore

Sharon's description: 'Kelly has wobblers'. Translation: Kelly can be very dramatic and have tantrums

Collections: Chairs, especially ones from the 1960s and 1970s

Education: Kelly left high school in California and earned her GED (General Education Development Certificate)

KELLY'S FAVES

COLOUR: Pink

BANDS: The Strokes, White Stripes, T-Rex, Blondie

CD: The Strokes' Is This It

BLACK SABBATH SONG: 'Paranoid'

TV SHOW: The Brady Bunch

FOOTWEAR: Her bunny slippers

HAIR COLOUR: Electric pink (right now)

CHAIR: Her bubble chair, which hangs from her bedroom ceiling

PASTIME: Shopping (she takes after her mum!)

SCHOOL SUBJECTS: Science and history

FASHION DESIGNERS: Zandra Rhodes, Helmut Lang

KIND OF BOY: 'I like smelly boys. I'm obsessed with the lead singer of the Strokes because he's a smelly rock star, and I love that.'

ACTORS: Ewan McGregor, Matthew Lillard

CITY: New York

✠ Jack's Basics

Real name: Jack Sabbath Osbourne

Birthday: November 8, 1985

Birthplace: England

Current US residence: Beverly Hills, California

Height: 5' 8"

Parents: Ozzy and Sharon Osbourne

Siblings: Aimee and Kelly

Sharon's description: 'Jack is kind of the oddball at school.'

Celebrity friends: Elijah Wood, pro skater Jason Dill

Most valuable book: A first edition of *The Lord of the Rings*

Collections: Toothbrushes – he has one for every day of the week

Instrument: Drums

Career goal: Music producer – right now he is working with Epic Records as a talent scout and is developing the group Delusion.

JACK'S FAVES

COLOUR: Black

BAND: Tool – Jack has seen the band in concert over 20 times

CD: Tool's Aenima

BEATLE ALBUM: Revolver

BLACK SABBATH SONG: 'Sympton of the Universe'

DOG: Lola, the bulldog

FASHION DESIGNERS: Hurley, DVS shoes – both companies have made Jack a spokesman for them – but he also likes vintage army surplus

PHRASE: 'It's a good time'

SPORT: Surfing – 'I'm scared to death of eight-foot waves, and I try to paddle before they crash over me. But it's fun!'

✠ Didja' Know?

★ Ozzy's first band was named Approach.

★ Heavy metal man Ozzy admits he likes Creed 'because they can sing!'

★ MTV paid the Osbournes $20,000 for each of the 10 episodes of the first season of their series. It's reported they will receive around $20 million for the second season. The second season takes place at their home in Buckinghamshire, Welders House.

★ There were 12 cameras in the house taping everything Ozzy and his clan did during the first season of *The Osbournes*.

★ Ozzy has a happy face tattooed on each knee to cheer him up when he wakes up in the morning.

★Sharon says she picked July 4 to be their wedding day so Ozzy would never forget it!

★At Ozzy's March 28, 1992 concert at Irvine Meadows in Laguna Hills, California, the metal madman invited the audience to join him on stage – it caused $100,000 in damages!

★Sharon Osbourne was named one of *People* magazine's '50 Most Beautiful People' in May 2002.

★Ozzy was the Fox News Channel's guest of honour at the annual White House Correspondents Association dinner. President George W. Bush declared that Ozzy was his mother's favourite performer.

★Ten of Ozzy's thirteen solo albums have gone multi-platinum.

★Jack has a teddy bear in his bedroom.

★ Kelly still sucks her thumb when she sleep

★ Ozzy had a hard time in school because he is severely dyslexic – and doctors had yet to understand the condition.

★ The Osbournes' house includes a home cinema, a tropical design pool, a jacuzzi and a billiards room.

★ When Sharon travels she usually brings Maggie, one of her Japanese Chin dogs.

★ The Osbournes' kitchen has four stoves, but they only use the one.

★ Kelly gets embarrassed when Ozzy and Sharon snuggle and kiss in public. Why? 'You're too old!' she tells her parents.

★ The Osbournes have been looking to buy an

apartment in New York City, but word has it that they've been turned down by several residents' associations . . . maybe because of their high profile lifestyle!

★Sharon made *The Times'* list of the one-hundred wealthiest women in Great Britain.

★Ozzy got his star on the Hollywood Walk of Fame on April 12, 2002.

★Sharon might be getting a new dog – it's a new breed and is the world's smallest. It's about the size of a grapefruit!

★Jack was once really keen on Shakespearean acting.

★You can now buy *The Osbournes* collectibles – from clothes to dolls. Sharon has approval on every bit of merchandise.

★In June 2002 the Osbournes released the CD, *The Osbourne Family Album*. Included is Kelly's debut song and cover rendition of Madonna's 'Papa Don't Preach', plus:

☆'Crazy Train' by Pat Boone
☆'Dreamer' by Ozzy Osbourne
☆'You Really Got Me' by The Kinks
☆'Snowblind' by System of a Down
☆'Imagine' by John Lennon
☆'Drive' by The Cars
☆'Good Souls' by Starsailor
☆'Mirror Image' by Dillusion
☆'Wonderful Tonight' by Eric Clapton
☆'Mama, I'm Coming Home'
    by Ozzy Osbourne
☆'Crazy Train' by Ozzy Osbourne
☆'Family System' by Chevelle

✠ CHAPTER ELEVEN
The First Ten Episodes – at a Glance

Here's a rundown of the Top Ten (okay, the first and only ten from season one) that kicked off *The Osbournes* phenomenon! All of them take place in Beverly Hills.

The show started with an intro to the family: dad, aka Ozzy, mum Sharon, daughter Kelly, 17, and their son Jack, 16. Viewers realized three things immediately: a) this is an unconventional family who truly loves one another b) why MTV uses those bleeping noises throughout the show, and c) this is a family worth checking out every week!

The dogs have gone 'mad.' Jack can't seem to control his favourite dog, Lola. She soils the carpet and chews everything in sight. Sharon has had enough. She calls a dog psychologist. But the soiling persists.

Ozzy promotes his new album. Jack gets shipped off to summer camp, but returns because he doesn't fit in. Kelly celebrates her seventeenth birthday and plucks up the courage to confess to her parents that she's got a tattoo. Needless, to say Ozzy and Sharon are not pleased.

This is the one where the family experiences a 'confrontation' with the neighbour and a ham is tossed over the fence.

Kelly and Mum go on a mega-shopping spree. And Ozzy freaks when Sharon books him for another show the following night. The Prince of Darkness seems to be furious. But all is forgotten when Ozzy is seen 'rockin it up' on stage.

Ozzy fractures a leg whilst performing on stage. There's trouble at home too when Ozzy and Sharon lay down the law with Kelly and Jack. They've been partying all-night and now they must pay – they've got a curfew.

 It's 'turkey time' at the Osbournes'. The family sits down for a Thanksgiving feast that includes stuffing and name calling – all you would expect from this fun-loving bunch.

 Meet Jason Dill – Jack's skateboarder friend, who happens to overstay his welcome at the Osbournes'. But Jason isn't the only one in the doghouse. Lola (the dog) has been up to her old tricks again!

 'Tis the season to be Ozzy! Ozzy and the family celebrate Christmas in style. For Sharon this involves shopping! Ozzy reflects on the modest way he used to celebrate Christmas as a child.

Ozzy finally gets a star on the Hollywood Walk of Fame. The family beams with pride. The episode ends with a montage of clips from the season.

✠ CHAPTER TWELVE
What Lies Ahead for the Osbourne Offspring?

The future for Kelly and Jack is brighter these days than the Day-Glo colours of their hair. Just glance at a news-stand and you're bound to find their faces on the covers of several magazines.

With at least two more seasons of *The Osbournes* secure under a multimillion-dollar contract negotiated by Sharon – thanks, Mum! – it's all these teenagers can do to keep up with the demand for them on the talk-show circuit.

And there's more to come: with the series soundtrack already in stores and a DVD box set of the first season inevitable, the merchandising craze of *The Osbournes* is just beginning.

Along the way America, and the rest of the world, is falling in love with its new It Girl and Boy. Kelly's ivory skin, sweet smile and genuine manner – not to mention her impeccable style – have won over viewers young and old. She's already proven that she's a natural in front of the camera, and possesses the poise and grace to be a much-endeared television personality. Let's face it, she can even make us want to hear 'Papa Don't Preach' again! Before recording the song, Kelly told the E! network, 'I didn't choose the song. My mum did and asked me to do it. I'm kind of crapping myself because I don't think I'm a very good singer.' But at the 2002 MTV Movie Awards, her performance was more hotly anticipated than bad-boy rapper Eminem's. She recorded the early Madonna hit with Incubus for *The Osbournes* soundtrack and is in talks with Epic Records about releasing a full CD. Maybe she'll start acting in movies, too.

Charming young Jack, meanwhile, is well on his way to realizing many of his dreams: he's a talent scout for one of the industry's biggest labels, a co-ordinator of the Second Stage at Ozzfest, and he's starting to set up his own record label. He can play the drums, too! His passion for music and inherent gift for business, as well as his social skills, make him destined to follow in the footsteps of his mother and grandfather and become one of rock 'n' roll's most powerful managers. Jack, the Hollywood supermogul? One thing's for sure: with hair like his, we know he's going to be huge. Well, OK, the hair and the *charm*.

Whatever the future holds for these two young superstars, one thing is for sure: Kelly and Jack will enjoy the love and support of their entire family, especially their doting mum and dad. Theirs may be an unconventional household, but this intriguing, close-knit family have captured our imaginations – and our hearts.

In fact, want to know what this autumn's hottest t-shirt proclaims?

'[BLEEP] MY FAMILY! I'M MOVING IN WITH THE OSBOURNES.'